ADAM L.S.

The Class

To all my students, you teach me something new every single day. - Adam L.S.

Remain teachable. - Adam L.S.

Contents

I

Chapter 1: The Flow

For Us

I can, you can, we can,
  for us all.

A striking sign of our times,
  are here, in our ideals, our origins.

We are worthy.
  This is for me, for you, for us.

Adam L.S.

Maybe

I was over and above proud…
    Of the loyalty.
    Of the common traditions.

Recognizing our higher power, the gifts.

We both serve.
    We recognize our purpose.
    We strive to do our best.

Soulmates?

Adam L.S.

We Are

We are free.
　We are a collection.
　We are something.

Adam L.S.

Probably

Is our purpose that clear?
  Protect, serve, create, and be responsible?

Adam L.S.

Nah

I asked to do His will...
  and then I wondered, what can I do to help?

Probably just a coincidence.

Adam L.S.

Grow & Play

Like plants, our minds grow.

Freedom is surely an ingredient,
    in preserving this instrument.

Adam L.S.

40

It's all a balancing act,
  isn't it?

Just two scoops.
  Just one basket.
  Just 3 hours.

Just not that easy.
  Or, is it?

Adam L.S.

Will

Good will.
His will.

My will is now His will.

Adam L.S.

Fly

Freedom preserved.

Freedom lost,
    freedom threatened,
    freedom destroyed.

Freedom created.

Adam L.S.

You & Me

I learned co-operation.
   It helped.

All the activities,
   requiring co-operation.

Not yoga so much, but that's nice too.

Adam L.S.

Smooth Talker

Those words,
    were so effective.

That speech,
    made a difference.

This relationship,
    requires communication.

Adam L.S.

Map

Steps…
   Actions..
   Communication…

The community is getting better.
   The world is getting better.

Which direction are we heading?

Adam L.S.

Transfer

The attraction…
  The belief…
  The interest…

In myself,
  Had to be transferred to them.

This must be my purpose,
  not tomorrow, but today.

I had to be led by good will, His will.

Adam L.S.

Frontiers

This was a new frontier,
   this knowledge and understanding.

The relief, possibilities, achievements.
   It takes action.

I improved, improve,
   I now cherish each moment in time.

Adam L.S.

Light Weight

My performance today is essential,
    for myself, my community, for tomorrow.

Adam L.S.

Discuss

I had to learn to communicate,
   to discuss the issues.

I had to become organized,
   to be free of the clutter.

Adam L.S.

Endless Service

Endless circumstances,
    however, I know my role now.

I'll be of service,
    all the time.

Adam L.S.

Changing

Classic,
   wanting to turn back the clock.

Impossible,
   so I began paying attention.

I'm now fond of the truth,
   in everything.

I've changed,
   these hands are strikingly beautiful.

Adam L.S.

CAPS LOCK

The supreme…
    Compliment.
    Enemy.
    System.

I had to develop…
    Intellect.
    Goals.
    Movement.

This emphasized my freedom.

Adam L.S.

A+

Principles,
     changed, unchanged.

Holding hope.
   Sharpening mind & body.

This assignment is extremely elaborate.

Adam L.S.

Life

I had to protect it,
    I reached out for it for so long.

Promoting my own freedom,
    was my own revival.

Adam L.S.

About Time

There is a notable difference,
    confidence, action,
        it feels right.

In favor of,
    myself, others, this world.

Adam L.S.

Flower

Straight to the root,
  of me, the problem.

Change, growth, freedom,
  the nutrients for it all.

Farewell weeds of reluctance.

Adam L.S.

Oh

Surrender,
    this pertains to freedom, anyway.

Adam L.S.

Bound

There's freedom, and then there's freedom,
  I thought I was free,
  but I couldn't stop.

Physical freedom, is separate from mental freedom.
  There were so many restrictions.

So many chains.

Adam L.S.

View

From there, that view,
  I imagined something different.

Was it a delusion?

Adam L.S.

Lock

I didn't remember the combination,
    or it was changed.

I'd never see those photos again.

Adam L.S.

It's Not

Is it guaranteed?
  Freedom?

I can walk to the store.
  But I cannot leave this place.

Adam L.S.

Condominium

In that condo,
  I was a piece of work, scrap, junk, simply shit.

There was death,
  I could not find freedom.

A conversation took place,
  even though I was alone.

And here I am, today.

Adam L.S.

Drama

Dramatic episodes galore…

No grounds,
  no principles.

Adam L.S.

Something Special

I had such a strong contempt for life,
    there was no higher value to any of it.

Was I indispensable?
    Could I get free?

One day, something special happened,
    I paid attention to life.

Adam L.S.

Spectrum

War,
   for control.

Deprived,
   of love.

Freedom,
   sought after.

No limits…?

Adam L.S.

Big Time

I manipulated,
   I lied,
   I ran…

I was scared, not present and insane.

Adam L.S.

Drums

I wasn't in a cage,
    should I be?

I wasn't growing,
    could I?

I wasn't growing,
    or was I?

It definitely had an effect,
    so now I hunt, for freedom.

Adam L.S.

Butthead

I infringed,
 I refused,
 I stole…

Their freedom.

Adam L.S.

Air

I was conditioned…

To be free,
   to be loved,
   to be me.

Adam L.S.

Watch Out

These arrangements dominated,
    my mind, my life.

I was not free,
    but I soon would be.

Adam L.S.

LMAO

Authority…
　Power…
　Property…

Whatever, man.
　You do you.

Adam L.S.

Swivel

Vote.
   Observe.
   Chuckle.
   Live.
   Swivel.

Keep going.

Adam L.S.

I Hope So

The masses…
   Their well being…

Can we evoke the welfare for all?

Adam L.S.

No Cage

Freeing myself of it all,
   so that I could be free.

Meant I could fly,
   I flew away.

Adam L.S.

Yes

Welfare & freedom?
   Yes.

Adam L.S.

Me

My analysis and emphasis,
    of those days…

Made me who I am today,
    and who I'll be tomorrow.

Adam L.S.

New

The ground shifted,
    I found a new footing.

Adam L.S.

Unnecessary Interruption

So many failures,
  outright disappointing.

Implications. Confusion…

So much unwillingness,
  outright illogical.

Adam L.S.

Life

All of it…

The time,
    the development,
    the connection,
    the questions.

The freedom to choose.

Adam L.S.

The Match

I wrestled with it,
  the situation was powerful.

There were no constraints.
  There were no alternatives.

The outcome would affect my goals.
  The outcome affected my values.

Adam L.S.

This Is New

My assignment,
   was my freedom.

This realms philosophy,
   was foreign to me.

As an imperfect being,
   this realm was perfect.

Adam L.S.

Court

Bad and good people,
    the same…

Who is judging?
    Who carries the scale?

Adam L.S.

Vault

I volunteered…
    I wasn't a victim…
    I was uncertain…

I was afraid.

Adam L.S.

Perpetuity

Provided…

We fed each other.
  We laughed.
  We cried, daily.
  We did so much together.
  We cooperated with each other.
  We needed directions though.

The day came, we were completely lost,
  we were fed up.

Adam L.S.

Bye

Coordinated coercion consists…
    Of a massive ego.

Present!

Just stop, dude.

Adam L.S.

People

My society!
　　Or, the society?
　　Our, society?

My life.
　　His society.
　　His will.

Adam L.S.

Exchange Rate

My exchanges,
   were always beneficial,
   to me.

Without coercion,
   we could both benefit.

Adam L.S.

Transactional

Too many to count,
    and I like numbers, and counting.

I like puzzles,
    but this was too complex.

I was rendered useless,
    my actions were ineffective.

I lost count.

Adam L.S.

No Clue

Speak,
  be precise.

These questions need answering.

Spell it out,
  in detail.

Adam L.S.

I Was The Majority

Power and freedom don't mix.
  I had become a dictator, and kept to my castle.

Adam L.S.

Below Deck

There were so many underlying arguments.

I lacked belief,
   that this would work.

I did not know the rules,
   deep breathes.

Someone had to umpire,
   and interpret this situation.

Adam L.S.

Treat You Right

Enforcing love,
   such a powerful substance.
   The most powerful substance.

There's no question,
   there's no end to the questions.

Don't interfere.

Adam L.S.

Survival Mechanism

Don't coerce.
  I'm not.
  You are.

Freedom is only possible without it.
  I believed it was the other way around.

Adam L.S.

Not An Act

I lost balance,
    they checked on me.

This system was busted,
    that system just smiled…

Confused.

Adam L.S.

Bankrupt

It was there, in frustration and fear,
  I was unable to decentralize those feelings from joy and love.

I was not the outstanding leader I thought I was.
  The expense was the joy…

And the love.

Adam L.S.

Focus

It was inevitable,
  so I'd have to concentrate…

It seemed so abstract,
  so it was hypothetical…

It mattered more than anything,
  so I kept going.

Adam L.S.

Acceptance

Another radical change,
 like last year.

I'm persuaded that I am now an advocate for peace.
 Wbu?

Adam L.S.

Inside Us All

They raised up,
   their hands,
   their might.

They may have initiated the problem,
   but they have the solution.

Adam L.S.

Always

It had to be public,
   why hide?

It's the truth
   it's love.

Published.

Adam L.S.

Initiate

Where do I begin?
  How did this all get started?

It's beautiful,
  don't you think?

Adam L.S.

VIP

My next venture,
    would not be so vicious.

This volume…

Victory.

Adam L.S.

You

I stretched,
  my imagination.

To keep up with you.

Adam L.S.

It's Right There

Give it your all?
  To whomever asks?

To keep it we have to give it away.

Adam L.S.

Indeed

The price is high,
    but there's an unlimited supply.

Sacrifice is appropriate,
    for freedom,
    for love.

Adam L.S.

That's Life

I was so irresponsible,
   so silly.

I was so young.
   so immature.

I faced life's difficulties,
   so be it.

Adam L.S.

Unknown

The question was just hanging there,
   suspended above.

The answer was often desirable,
   but not always.

Adam L.S.

Here We Go!

My previous chapter,
   and the role I played…
   Was, so different.

I made notes.
   and this chapter I…
   Well, you'll see.

Adam L.S.

Consensus

So many alternatives,
  So many ineffective decisions.

Often these operations destroyed lines of communication.

Adam L.S.

Clearly Illogical

There was another objection,
  am I really justifying the means?

Probably.

Adam L.S.

Resources

With respect…

This may be impossible.
    We must protect ourselves.

Adam L.S.

Joint Action

I wanted to reconcile.
   These channels would inevitably be strained.

I wanted cohesion.
   These channels could stabilize.

Adam L.S.

Common

Delicate people,
  delicate hearts,
  delicate threads.

Adam L.S.

Playbook

Rule makers,
 day to day

Play makers,
 day to day.

Adam L.S.

Mindful

Enforcing good conditions,
    when we have differing interpretations.

Adam L.S.

The Problem

Trading ideas,
   with terms and conditions.

The sterling dilemma,
   with techniques required to connect.

Adam L.S.

Solution

Neglect,
   the most serious threat to freedom,
   causing an outbreak of war.

Controls,
   to solve the balance,
   seems innocuous.

Spiraling
   so destructive,
   so just love.

Adam L.S.

The Cure

The cure seemed vastly worse,
    than the actual disease.

Adam L.S.

The Disguise

This wasn't a flimsy disguise,
  there was something new under the sun.

Adam L.S.

Conference

This series is long delayed,
   I had a conference with Him.

This series is because of Him,
   here we go!

Adam L.S.

Director

The subsequent years…
  Directed by me.

The subsequent principles…
  Directed by me.

The subsequent problems…
  Directed by me.

Adam L.S.

Them

Indebted to them,
    they invited me in,

A friendship formed,
    this one is for them.

Adam L.S.

So Responsible

Responsible participants,
   their deep interest,
   their nquenchable intellectual enthusiasm,
   their ability to correct many errors…

Of my life.

Adam L.S.

Flex

The philosophy,
   that inner strength exists.

Do we use it today?
   Or tomorrow?

Adam L.S.

Madman

A line had been drawn,
　　madman, child or…

Was I ready to walk on paternalistic grounds?
　　Was I responsible enough?

Or was I part of the others.

Adam L.S.

Not So Fast

I was designated as lost,
    I was designated as irresponsible,
    I was designated as another case of psychosis, schizophrenic or both.

The case was closed,
    The decision was made...

Just kidding,
    look at me now.

Adam L.S.

Always

Make arrangements,
　be willing to rearrange those arrangements...

It's for their care,
　their development.

You must provide for your children.

Adam L.S.

Key

Pardon... Me. You.

  Acceptance. Empathy. Gratitude. Strength. Peace. Love. Faith. Willingness... Is key.

Adam L.S.

The Manuscript

These scraps of truths,
    weathered.

Enough of them gathered, pieced together,
    and the page read, "Preface."

Adam L.S.

Books

It's time for some revisions…
   These bits and pieces have to go…
   Editing these chapters is necessary…
   I have the pen..
   He calls the shots…
   It's time…

His will.

Adam L.S.

Notes

Notes

Notes

Notes

Also by Adam L.S.

The Fellowship is poetry exploring addiction, and the Fellowship that is available to the recovering addict.

The Fellowship
Coming soon!

www.ingramcontent.com/pod-product-compliance
Lightning Source LLC
Chambersburg PA
CBHW071920120726
48001CB00005B/1809